GW01246526

Original title:
The Snow Glimmer

Author: Paula Raudsepp
ISBN HARDBACK: 978-9916-79-669-6
ISBN PAPERBACK: 978-9916-79-670-2
ISBN EBOOK: 978-9916-79-671-9

Frostflake Lullabies Under Moonlit Dreams

In the hush of night, soft whispers call,
Frosty flakes dance, a silvery sprawl.
Moonlight glimmers, a tranquil beam,
Cradling dreams in a gentle stream.

Stars are blinking, a tender sight,
Covered in blankets of purest white.
Snowflakes twirl like a waltz in air,
Weaving wishes without a care.

Nature's magic, a soothing balm,
In winter's embrace, the world feels calm.
Lullabies sung by the sighing pines,
Cradling hearts where hope aligns.

In every flake, a story spun,
Of laughter, love, and warmth in sun.
Kissed by the moon, they softly gleam,
Carrying us into a dream.

So close your eyes, let the world drift far,
With frostflake lullabies, we'll follow the star.
In this still wonder, let worries cease,
Embrace the night, find your peace.

Radiance Upon the Frozen Earth

In winter's grasp, the silence sings,
A world transformed, as beauty clings.
Soft glows emerge, from frostbite's grip,
A crystalline dance, where shadows slip.

The stars above, like diamonds twirl,
Each breath a mist, as dreams unfurl.
In twilight's glow, the earth wears white,
A tranquil scene, bathed in soft light.

Icicles Catching Moonbeams

Hanging low, like daggers bright,
They glimmer softly in the night.
Each drop awaits the dawn's warm grace,
A fleeting touch of light's embrace.

The moonlight weaves through branches bare,
As whispers curl in frosty air.
They shimmer faintly, a silver thread,
In winter's realm, where dreams are bred.

Luminous Veil of the Frost

A blanket soft upon the ground,
Where nature rests, and peace is found.
Each crystal flake, a story told,
In whispers etched, in silver cold.

Beneath the glow of starlit skies,
The moon bestows its softest sighs.
A breathtaking sight in night's embrace,
As dreams are born in this pure space.

Glacial Kisses at Dusk

As shadows stretch and daylight fades,
The icy breath of winter wades.
A gentle touch upon the cheek,
Where silence sings and hearts may speak.

The colors shift in purple hues,
As daylight bids its soft adieu.
Each glacial kiss, a secret shared,
In dusk's soft glow, we are ensnared.

The Radiance of Each Snowflake

In the hush of winter's breath,
Snowflakes dance, a silent death.
Fragile crystals touch the ground,
A myriad of forms abound.

They glisten bright in morning light,
Whispers of joy in sheer delight.
Each one unique, a fleeting grace,
Nature's art, a soft embrace.

Falling gently from the sky,
Like a lullaby passing by.
In their fall, no haste nor pride,
They blanket earth, a pure white tide.

As time passes, they will melt,
But the warmth of joy is felt.
In memory, they leave their mark,
A fleeting glow in winters dark.

Chasing the Glimmering Mirage

Across the desert, heatwaves rise,
A shimmering dance before our eyes.
Hopes entwined with grains of sand,
Dreams of waters, soft and grand.

Footsteps echo on dusty land,
Each breath a wish, each touch a hand.
In the distance, a vision gleams,
Reality blurred with vibrant dreams.

A mirage sways, elusive grace,
Chasing shadows in endless space.
With the sunburnt sky aglow,
Seeking truth in shimmering flow.

Hearts aflame with transient light,
Living fiercely, souls take flight.
In pursuit of what seems to be,
The heart knows well, it longs to see.

Winter's Stunning Illusion

Whispers of frost on window panes,
Winter weaves its silvery chains.
A landscape dressed in purest white,
An enchanting world, a wondrous sight.

Each branch adorned with frosty lace,
Every shadow finds its place.
In stillness, nature sleeps, serene,
A breathtaking hush grips the scene.

Crimson berries 'neath the snow,
A gentle promise, life will grow.
Nature's beauty, wrapped in cold,
A tale of warmth in silence told.

Yet as the sun begins to rise,
Winter fades, the beauty sighs.
In melting ice, a glimpse of spring,
The cycle turns, new joys to bring.

Moonbeams on a Frozen Lake

Under the glow of silver light,
Moonbeams dance on the lake so bright.
Crystals shimmer on frozen waves,
A tapestry of dreams, it saves.

Stars reflect in a tranquil guise,
Echoes of night under vast skies.
Silent whispers of nature's tune,
Cascading down beneath the moon.

Footsteps trace the icy shore,
Every path a tale of yore.
A realm where time stands still and waits,
A crafted pause by gentle fates.

In this moment, hearts align,
Lost in the beauty, pure, divine.
Beneath the moon, dreams have taken flight,
In the stillness of the winter night.

A Dance of Frozen Light

Beneath the starry veil, they twirl,
Whispers of winter in a whirl.
Shimmering pathways glisten bright,
In the embrace of frozen light.

The night unveils its crystal show,
As shadows play in the moon's glow.
Step by step, they grace the night,
In this enchanting, frozen sight.

Glistening flakes begin to fall,
Each one unique, nature's call.
They dance and float, a soft delight,
Creating magic, pure and white.

Leaves of silver, branches bare,
Whispered secrets fill the air.
Hearts entwined in the soft white,
Lost together, in the night.

Waltzing through the silent trees,
The world at rest, a gentle breeze.
Together bound, hearts take flight,
In this dance of frozen light.

Radiant Blankets of White

A crispness fills the early morn,
While nature's beauty is reborn.
Blankets soft, the earth they drape,
In radiant white, a perfect shape.

Footsteps crunch on powdery trails,
As stories linger, winter tales.
Every flake a tale to tell,
In radiant white, they weave a spell.

Hills adorned in shimmering cloth,
Wrapped in dreams, they softly swath.
Trees stand tall, like guardians, bright,
In the glow of a tranquil night.

Children laughing, faces aglow,
Creating magic in the snow.
With every toss, a squeal of delight,
In this wonder, pure and white.

As dusk arrives, soft hues ignite,
A canvas painted, day to night.
Whispers of peace take their flight,
In radiant blankets of white.

Sparkling Secrets in the Chill

In the quiet of the frozen wood,
Magic lingers where it once stood.
Secrets hold in each soft flake,
Sparkling brightly for winter's sake.

Beneath the frost, the whispers creep,
Nature's heart, in silence deep.
Crystals twinkle, shy and bright,
Hiding dreams in the chill of night.

From branches high, the cold winds call,
Dancing softly, a gentle thrall.
Each breath a mist, in frozen light,
Sparkling secrets, soft and slight.

As twilight fades and shadows play,
The world transformed, in soft display.
A symphony of silvered sight,
Whispers echo, in the night.

Gathered round, the stars take flight,
Igniting dreams in cosmic light.
In the chill, our hearts unite,
With sparkling secrets shining bright.

Ethereal Frost on Sleeping Earth

A hush has fallen, calm and deep,
Nature cradles, softly asleep.
Ethereal frost, a tender shroud,
Covers gently, like a cloud.

Moonlight dances on the trees,
Casting shadows in the breeze.
Crystalline whispers fill the night,
Unveiling wonders, pure delight.

Fields adorned, a quiet grace,
In silver beauty, nature's face.
Dreams are woven, soft and girth,
In the arms of sleeping earth.

Every breath, a world so still,
With frostiness, the air does thrill.
A spell is cast as hearts find mirth,
In this moment on the earth.

Awake we'll be when spring comes near,
But for now, we hold it dear.
In the stillness, beauty's worth,
Ethereal frost on sleeping earth.

Dances of Light Across the Ice

Beneath the moon's soft glow,
Colors shimmer, ebb and flow.
Whispers float on chilly air,
As shadows twist in silver flare.

Glistening trails on frozen ground,
Nature's beauty all around.
With each step, the echoes play,
A serenade of night and day.

Skaters glide like fleeting dreams,
Through the silence, laughter beams.
In a world where time stands still,
Magic spins with each new thrill.

Gales of frost kiss rosy cheeks,
In this realm, each moment peaks.
The dance of light, a fleeting spark,
Illuminates the winter dark.

As dawn breaks, the colors fade,
Yet memories in hearts are laid.
The ice remains, a canvas bare,
Until again, the dancers dare.

Brilliant Frosty Sonnet

Crystals twinkle on the trees,
Winter's breath, a chill that frees.
Morning light breaks soft and bright,
Painting landscapes pure and white.

Every branch adorned with care,
Sparkles gleam in crisp, cold air.
Nature's jewels glint and shine,
A frigid beauty, so divine.

Footprints tread on fresh-swept snow,
A fleeting path where soft winds blow.
Silent moments stretched in time,
Echoes linger, caught in rhyme.

As the sun sinks low and red,
Dreams unfold where others tread.
In this frosty paradise,
Life's reflections, cold yet nice.

A fleeting glance, a day's retreat,
In winter's arms, the heart's warm beat.
With every breath, the world stands still,
Brilliant frosty dreams fulfill.

When the World Turns to Silver

With twilight's veil, the night descends,
A silvery calm, the day now ends.
Shadows blend with the cool moonlight,
Painting visions, soft and bright.

Ice crystals form a frozen lace,
Blanketing the world in grace.
Each breath released, a misty sigh,
As the stars adorn the sky.

Moments linger, time slows down,
In this silvery, serene gown.
Whispers carried on the breeze,
Embrace the stillness, hearts at ease.

Nature's hush, a sacred sound,
As dreams awaken all around.
In this realm, where magic swirls,
A silver dance, as night unfurls.

With every pulse, the night inspires,
A gentle warmth ignites the fires.
When the world turns soft and bright,
We find our peace in the silver light.

A Symphony of Ice and Stars

In the stillness of the night,
Stars above twinkle in flight.
Beneath the vast and velvet sky,
Whispers of frosty breezes sigh.

Melodies of ice, they ring,
Nature's choir begins to sing.
Each note drifts through frozen air,
A symphony beyond compare.

Footfalls echo on the frost,
In this wonderland, we're not lost.
Moments captured, hearts entwined,
In the harmony we find.

Luminous dance on sparkling ground,
In the quiet, joy is found.
Stars align, a cosmic show,
In unity, our spirits glow.

As dawn approaches, shadows flee,
Yet the music lingers free.
A symphony of night and day,
Forever in our hearts will stay.

Luminescent Trails of Winter's Breath

Footprints fade in the snowy night,
Glowing trails under pale moonlight.
Whispers of frost in the crisp, cold air,
Nature's canvas, so beautifully rare.

Branches glisten with a silvery sheen,
The world transformed, a magical scene.
Stars twinkle softly, a watchful sight,
Guiding hearts through the still of night.

Chill winds dance with a gentle grace,
As shadows waver in this quiet space.
Hushed secrets linger in the frost,
In winter's arms, we find what's lost.

Each breath lingers, a mist in the dark,
Echoes of laughter, a fleeting spark.
As the world sleeps under blankets of white,
Hope glimmers softly, ready for flight.

A symphony plays in the cold, crisp air,
Harmony found in an icy affair.
With every heartbeat, magic unfurls,
In the luminescent dance of winter's swirls.

Whispers of Ice Beneath the Stars

Silent woods where shadows creep,
Moonlit glimmers where secrets keep.
Stars unveil in the ebony night,
Whispers of ice take their flight.

Beneath the surface, stories decay,
Forever frozen, they silently stay.
Frosty tendrils map the old ground,
In this stillness, lost voices resound.

Crystals shimmer with a ghostly hue,
Painting memories of days anew.
Each breath exhaled, a delicate sigh,
As memories dance and time passes by.

The sky reveals its infinite lore,
While the earth sleeps, we explore.
Through the quiet, soft echoes play,
Guiding lost souls on their way.

In the heart of winter, the stars awake,
The quiet truth behind every flake.
Where secrets linger and shadows play,
Whispers of ice shall lead the way.

Shining Carpets of Glacial Touch

Fields adorned in a blanket of snow,
A shimmering carpet set to glow.
Crystalline beauty spread far and wide,
Winter's magic, a watchful guide.

Each step whispers of stories untold,
As the winter sun casts its gold.
Frost-kissed leaves glimmer with cheer,
Nature's artwork, perfectly clear.

Underfoot, the crunch breaks the still,
Where time pauses, and dreams fulfill.
Dancing flakes in a waltz so sweet,
Every moment a gentle heartbeat.

Shadows play where the trees stand tall,
A story written through winter's call.
With each breath, new visions arise,
Reflecting stars in the winter skies.

We wander on this glacial thread,
Guided by warmth where hearts are led.
In the silence, a truth we clutch,
Life unfolds in a glorious touch.

Echoes of Magic on the Frozen Drift

Frosty air, a chill in the breeze,
Whispers of magic among the trees.
On frozen drifts, a tale begins,
As winter's song beckons, it spins.

Crystalline shards catch the light,
Sparkling whispers in the serene night.
Beneath silver skies, memories shout,
Inviting the dreamers to wander about.

Footfalls steady on this winter map,
Where a tranquil world invites a nap.
Echoes of laughter dance in the snow,
Tales of the past in the moon's soft glow.

Through shimmering fields of frost-kissed bliss,
Magic awakens in each icy kiss.
The universe breathes, its beauty unfurled,
Painting whispers that enchant the world.

Silent enchantments, a night so divine,
A path illuminated where stars align.
In the heart of winter, love drifts near,
Echoes of magic for all who hear.

Glimmering Shadows on Snow

Silent flakes fall from the sky,
Whispers of winter as they fly.
Beneath the moon's soft, glowing light,
Shadows dance in the calm of night.

Trees stand tall with branches bare,
Holding secrets in the air.
Each sparkle reflects the chill,
Glimmers of magic, quiet and still.

Footprints lead where few have gone,
Tracing paths until the dawn.
In the hush, our breath is seen,
Framed in frost, a wintry dream.

Let the world drift and unwind,
In this space, we're intertwined.
The shadows play, the echoes hum,
In glimmering snow, we become one.

Frosted Gleams of Joy

Morning light breaks through the frost,
Each ray glimmers, no moment lost.
Crystal branches catch the gleam,
In this world, I find my dream.

Joy is painted in shades of white,
With every breath, the heart feels light.
Snowflakes twirl, a soft ballet,
Frosted whispers, come what may.

Laughter echoes, children play,
Chasing snowflakes throughout the day.
Each flurry wraps us in delight,
Creating memories, pure and bright.

In every drift, a tale unfolds,
Frosted gleams, the warmth it holds.
Through winter's eye, we see the glow,
In every heartbeat, joy will flow.

Nature's art, so pure, divine,
In frozen canvases, we find.
With every step on snowy ground,
Frosted dreams, all around.

Silhouettes in a Glittering White

Against the snow, the figures stand,
Silent watchers of this land.
Shadows stretch, long and lean,
In this stillness, a sight serene.

Frosted glories cover the field,
Nature's beauty quietly revealed.
Every contour, every line,
In the white, a soft design.

Soft winds whisper through the trees,
Carrying tales on winter's breeze.
In this place, time seems to freeze,
While snowflakes dance with gentle ease.

Each silhouette tells a story,
Woven in winds, a hidden glory.
In quiet moments, we see the art,
Of glittering white, a soothing heart.

Together we stand, brave and bold,
In these shadows, warmth unfolds.
Embracing winter's soft embrace,
Silhouettes in this wondrous space.

Echoes of Winter's Breath

Through the pines, the breezes sing,
Echoes of joy that winter brings.
Frosted paths beneath our feet,
In the silence, our hearts meet.

Each breath steams in the chilly air,
Carried softly, our dreams laid bare.
Snowflakes twirl, a ballet supreme,
Echoing life in a crystal dream.

Branches bow with laden grace,
Nature's wonder in every space.
Every sound, each gentle sigh,
In winter's grasp, we learn to fly.

Together we wander, lost and found,
In the beauty of this white abound.
Echoes of laughter, warmth inside,
Winter's breath, our steadfast guide.

Let the chill embrace us near,
With every moment, dispelling fear.
In the echoes, our spirits dance,
Living in winter's sweet romance.

Shivering in Radiant Beauty

In the quiet of winter's breath,
Colors dance, but life feels leashed.
Branches bare, adorned in white,
A world wrapped in shimmering light.

Vibrant hues on frosted ground,
Silent whispers, beauty found.
Amidst the chill, a heart beats warm,
Wrapped in nature's gentle charm.

The sun peeks through, shy yet bold,
Casting sparkles, indirectly told.
Each moment brief, yet crystalline,
Within this frame, is where I dream.

Winds carry tales from afar,
Songs of warmth beneath the star.
In this shivering radiant glow,
I find the peace that winter knows.

Reflections dance on icy streams,
Carried softly, like fleeting dreams.
In the stillness, hearts ignite,
Shivering in radiant light.

Snowflakes' Graceful Ballet

Snowflakes twirl, a ballet grand,
Gracefully drifting, hand in hand.
Each unique, a story spun,
Under the light of a low-hung sun.

Pirouettes in softest air,
Falling gently without a care.
Whispers of frost, soft and sweet,
Painting the world, a grand retreat.

Between the trees where shadows play,
They gather close, then drift away.
In their dance, the silence sings,
A symphony of winter's wings.

Each flake a dream in fleeting flight,
Bringing magic to the night.
In the tapestry of the cold,
A tale of beauty, yet untold.

Together they swirl, a gentle night,
Choreographed in tranquil light.
In this graceful, snowy ball,
We find the joy within it all.

Frosted Dreams on the Horizon

On the horizon, the dawn breaks clear,
Frosted dreams whisper, drawing near.
A canvas painted in icy hues,
With every breath, the world renews.

Glistening fields in morning's glow,
Where the softest breezes blow.
Each blade of grass, a crystal wand,
Creating magic across the pond.

Dreams of winter linger low,
Amidst the white, new thoughts will grow.
Every shimmer holds a secret tight,
In their embrace, the day takes flight.

Mountains stand with a frozen stare,
Guardians of dreams caught in the air.
Beneath their watch, a tale unfolds,
Of frost and fire, of warmth and cold.

As daylight climbs, shadows creep,
Covering the landscape, thoughts to keep.
In every heartbeat, a precious sign,
Frosted dreams dance on the line.

Glimmering Icicles at Dusk

As dusk falls softly, shadows blend,
Icicles glimmer, nature's pen.
Writing stories in the fading light,
Of the passing day and coming night.

Each hanging shard a crystal flame,
Reflecting whispers, night's soft name.
They sway gently, like ancient chimes,
Marking moments, capturing times.

Underneath a blanket of stars,
The world feels close, with no more bars.
In their glow, I find the peace,
A tranquil moment, worries cease.

The chill wraps round, a cozy cloak,
Enveloping hearts, as stillness spoke.
In this hour, all feels profound,
Glimmering icicles, dreams unbound.

So here I stand, in awe and grace,
Witnessing nature's perfect face.
In dusk's embrace, my spirit flies,
With glimmering icicles lighting the skies.

Shimmering Nightfall

As twilight drapes the earth in blue,
The stars awaken, one by one,
Whispers of dreams float softly through,
Under the spell of the rising moon.

Shadows dance where secrets hide,
Gentle breezes sing their tune,
Embraced by night, the world feels wide,
In the glow of a silvered rune.

A flicker here, a shimmer there,
The heavens weave their magic light,
Guiding hearts with tender care,
Through the calm of the velvet night.

With every breath, a story's spun,
In this realm of soft delight,
Where all our worries come undone,
Bathed within the shimmering night.

So let the stars be our guide,
In a world where dreams take flight,
With hope and love forever tied,
Together we will greet the night.

Winter's Dazzling Reverie

Winter's breath, a crisp embrace,
The world adorned in purest white,
Each flake a dream with gentle grace,
As dawn unveils the morning light.

The frosty air, so sharp and clear,
It sparkles in the sun's warm glow,
Whispering secrets only we hear,
In soft, enchanted drifts of snow.

Footprints mark the path we tread,
Of laughter shared and joys unveiled,
Within this maze, our hearts are led,
Through winter's magic, we've not failed.

The night descends, the stars ignite,
A twinkling show of diamond bright,
In this reverie, hearts take flight,
Warmed by love against the cold's bite.

In the hush of the snowy trees,
Dreams gather like the falling snow,
Wrapped in winter's gentle freeze,
United in a dazzling glow.

Silvery Embrace of Cold

A silvery blanket covers all,
With every touch, the world is still,
As nature wraps in winter's thrall,
Time pauses, a serene chill.

Trees stand tall, their branches clad,
In icy crystals, shining bright,
Each beauty shared, a heart so glad,
In the quiet hush of the night.

Footsteps crunch on frozen ground,
Echoes of laughter fill the air,
Magic in every sound profound,
Lost in moments pure and rare.

With every breath, the frost bites deep,
Yet warmth resides within our hearts,
In this embrace, we take a leap,
Into the realm where nature starts.

So hold me close in winter's sway,
Together we shall face the cold,
In silvery dreams, we'll brightly play,
Finding warmth in tales untold.

Gleaming Veil of Winter's Calm

A gleaming veil of winter's night,
Cascades over the slumbering ground,
With every star that shines so bright,
A world transformed, beauty unbound.

The moonlight dances on the snow,
Creating sparkles, pure and white,
In this silence, the heart will grow,
Wrapped in dreams of soft twilight.

As frozen rivers lay to sleep,
And whispers weave through trees so bare,
In nature's arms, our worries leap,
To find solace in the cool air.

Through the woods, the shadows play,
Twinkling softly in the dark,
With winter's touch, we find our way,
In this calm, our spirits spark.

So let us wander side by side,
In the gleaming night, love shall warm,
Through winter's grace, we will abide,
Together safe from any storm.

Celestial Shards Cross the Ground

Stars scatter softly like seeds,
Across the night's vast, velvet field.
Whispers of dreams ride gentle winds,
As moonlight's glow begins to yield.

Fragments of cosmos drift and sway,
Crystallized glimmers on the earth.
Each moment a fleeting ballet,
A dance of wonder, a rebirth.

Light weaves through the tapestry,
Invisible threads, silent grace.
Every spark holds a mystery,
In the stillness, time finds its place.

In shadows, the universe winks,
Sparks of history, old and bright.
Celestial realms forge new links,
In the quiet embrace of night.

Gaze at the splendor up high,
Nature's canvas, vast and wide.
Celestial shards blushing the sky,
In their beauty, dreams abide.

Chilling Grace of Wandering Light

Flickers of frost on the edge of day,
Dancing softly, a delicate bite.
The chilling grace that leads astray,
A wandering light fills the night.

Shadows stretch long, the world holds its breath,
Whispers of silence mirror the stars.
Moments of warmth mingle with death,
Chilling grace, weave through our scars.

Ghostly figures, the frost does paint,
On rooftops, tree limbs, and winding lanes.
Nature's own art, a beautiful taint,
A winter's spell wrapped in refrains.

Each flake falls as a story untold,
A journey begun in the quiet of night.
Echoes of secrets, thus unfold,
In the chilling grace of wanderlight.

Illuminating paths we have known,
Casting shadows that softly cling.
In every sparkle, in every tone,
Chilling grace of the winter's fling.

Frostbite's Prismatic Touch

A breath so cold, it stings the air,
Frostbite's kiss, a cutting flair.
Colors woven in delicate freeze,
Nature's brush paints with such ease.

Crystals form in a beautiful haze,
Sparkle like diamonds in the dim light.
Each glimmer captures fleeting rays,
Frostbite's touch, a dazzling sight.

Frozen tendrils embrace the ground,
Whispers of winter, bold yet shy.
In this silence, beauty is found,
Underneath the cobalt sky.

A palette rich with hues of blue,
Nature's art, a masterpiece spun.
Frostbite's prismatic touch anew,
Refracting colors, one by one.

Through chill and shimmer, we behold,
The magic in the chilly air.
Frostbite's tales, in silence told,
Woven dreams beyond compare.

Whispered Wishes in White

In the quiet, snowflakes fall,
Whispered wishes float on the breeze.
Each flake a dream, a tiny call,
Embracing the world with gentle ease.

Covered in blankets of softest white,
Landscapes transform beneath the night.
The whispers of hopes in the frosty air,
In winter's embrace, we pause and care.

Glistening paths where memories tread,
Footprints fade in the blanket below.
Hushed secrets from hearts long dead,
In the tranquil hum of falling snow.

With each wish, a promise made,
Underneath the white, a chance to grow.
In fragile beauty, we are swayed,
Whispered wishes, a soft glow.

As dawn breaks, the world shines bright,
New dreams emerge, a sacred rite.
In the stillness, the heart takes flight,
Whispered wishes, forever in white.

Winter's Shining Heart

In the stillness of the night,
Snowflakes dance in soft delight,
Every whisper, every sigh,
Holds the winter's secret high.

Frosty breath upon the air,
Nature swathes in crystal flare,
Moonlight paints a world anew,
Glistening dreams in silver hue.

Branches draped in icy lace,
Time stands still in this embrace,
Echoes of a gentle chill,
Winter's heart, a peace to fill.

By the fire, warmth and glow,
Time to share what we all know,
Moments carved in frozen grace,
Winter's magic we embrace.

As dawn breaks with golden light,
Snowflakes shimmer, pure and bright,
In the heart of winter's spell,
A tale of love weaves and dwells.

The Magic of Frozen Light

Underneath a twilight sky,
Snowflakes fall, a soft goodbye,
Each one glimmers, pure and bright,
Casting dreams in silver light.

Icicles like crystal spears,
Whisper secrets, hold our fears,
In their depths, a world confined,
Frozen magic, intertwined.

Fields of white, a canvas vast,
Time flows gently, shadows cast,
Winds that carry stories far,
Highlighting wonders, like a star.

In the silence, hearts unite,
Bound by warmth, despite the night,
Shared moments, laughter's sound,
In this magic, love is found.

Glistening paths of frosted dreams,
Life unfolds in silver seams,
Every heartbeat, we ignite,
In the magic of frozen light.

A Shimmering Tapestry of Time

Threads of gold and silver spun,
Weave together, two as one,
Moments caught like evening dew,
In a quilt of memories true.

Seasons change, yet still they blend,
Time unfolds, a faithful friend,
In the tapestry we share,
Stories linger, woven care.

With each thread, a tale we tell,
Echoes of where we once fell,
In the fabric, joy and pain,
Together in the sun and rain.

Every stitch holds whispers dear,
Of laughter shared and silent tears,
Colors bright against the night,
A shimmering tapestry of light.

So let us gather, hold it tight,
Every memory, pure delight,
In this beauty, we will find,
Love's embrace in shared design.

Echoes of Light on Ice

In the hush of morning's glow,
Sunlight dances on the snow,
Every shimmer, every gleam,
Echoes softly like a dream.

Skates that glide on frozen streams,
Whirling like enchanted dreams,
In the silence, spirits soar,
Echoes whisper, wanting more.

Footprints trace a path of white,
Guiding hearts towards the light,
Each reflection, shimmering grace,
Crafts a moment, time and space.

Nature's canvas clear and bright,
Paints the world with pure delight,
In the still and crisp embrace,
Echoes of a tranquil place.

As evening falls, the stars ignite,
Holding dreams in soft twilight,
In the quiet, shadows play,
Echoes of light guide the way.

Celestial Glow Across Winter's Expanse

The moonlight bathes the silent night,
A shimmering veil, a soft delight.
Stars whisper secrets, calm and clear,
In winter's breath, the world is near.

Frost-kissed branches, silvered grace,
Nature's beauty, a tranquil space.
Each flake dances, a fleeting dream,
In the chill, all is as it seems.

Glistening snowflakes gently fall,
A soft hush blankets, calling all.
Wrapped in wonder, hearts behold,
The magic of winter, a tale untold.

Through the cold, we find our way,
Guided by starlight, night and day.
Celestial whispers lead us home,
Across the expanses where shadows roam.

Glimmering Gothic Spires of Frost

Upon the skyline, towers rise,
Gothic spires reach for snowy skies.
Frosted edges, intricate lace,
A haunting beauty, an elegant grace.

Moonlight dances on frozen stone,
Echoes of silence, a ghostly throne.
Each step taken on wintry ground,
Whispers of history in the sound.

Windows glimmer in the icy night,
Flickering dreams, a spectral light.
Shadows twist like stories untold,
In the chill of winter, hearts grow bold.

Beneath the spires, secrets lie,
In every corner, a silent sigh.
Glint of frost on weary knees,
A moment captured in the freeze.

Twilight's Radiance Above the Snow

As daylight fades, the twilight glows,
Painting the world in softest rose.
Snow blankets all in a hush profound,
Twilight whispers, beauty's found.

Glowing embers in a fading sky,
March of shadows, the day bids goodbye.
Colors cascade, a gentle flow,
Kissing the earth with the warmth of glow.

Each flake reflects the fading light,
Dancing softly, lost in flight.
Hearts stir gently, memories wake,
In twilight's arms, we softly ache.

Beneath the canvas of night's embrace,
We find our stillness, a sacred space.
Radiance lingers in whispers low,
Where the world rests, wrapped in snow.

Glistening Silhouettes in the Chilling Air

Silhouettes rise against the dawn,
Framed in frost, the world reborn.
Chilling air carries dreams anew,
In glistening whispers, the morning's hue.

Trees stand tall, cloaked in white,
Guardians of secrets that beckon night.
Each breath a fog, each moment rare,
In the stillness, magic hangs in air.

Footsteps crunch on the icy ground,
Echoes of laughter, joy unbound.
Glistening moments shine so bright,
Illuminated by the soft, pale light.

A canvas painted with dreams and sighs,
Underneath the sprawling skies.
Here in the chill, we find our place,
In glistening silhouettes, we find our grace.

Frosty Reflections in Quiet Woods

In the stillness of the night,
Whispers dance on frozen air,
Moonlight weaves a silver thread,
Through branches bare and fair.

Footsteps crunch on sparkling ground,
Nature's breath, a soft embrace,
Echoes of a world profound,
In this serene, enchanted space.

Icicles hang like chandeliers,
Glistening in the starlit glow,
Each shimmering drop holds time,
In the woods where shadows flow.

A sigh from trees, a gentle sound,
Frosty secrets softly kept,
In the heart of winter's hold,
Where the wild things dream and slept.

Reflections shimmer, glimpses rare,
In the quiet, life reclaims,
A tapestry of frost and air,
Whispering the woods' own names.

Halos of Ice and Light

Beneath the canopy so vast,
Halos form with each soft breath,
Draped in crystals, worlds collide,
Nature's light conquers death.

Every flake a work of art,
Glittering softly in the dark,
Illuminating hidden paths,
With each twinkling, vivid spark.

Frozen lakes, a mirror bright,
Reflecting dreams of days gone by,
Sunrise casts a golden hue,
As shadows dance and spirits fly.

Chill of night, the warmth of dawn,
Colors merge to show the way,
In this realm where time stands still,
Halos beckon, gently sway.

Moments linger, slow and pure,
Each breath a note in winter's song,
Whispers echo, drawing close,
In this place where we belong.

Crystal Dreams in Twilight

As twilight falls on frosted ground,
Dreams begin to take their flight,
Shadows stretch and softly blend,
In the calm embrace of night.

Crystalline whispers fill the air,
Echoes of the day's retreat,
Stars arise like distant hopes,
Mapping dreams with silver feet.

The horizon glows with softest tones,
Crimson sighs meet sapphire blue,
Every hue a story tells,
Of the journeys that we pursue.

In this crystal world adorned,
Time unfurls with each soft breath,
Twilight wraps the earth in peace,
Whispers shared, no fear of death.

Beneath the arch of fading light,
Hearts entwine in silent grace,
In the fabric of the dusk,
We find our truest, sacred space.

Wintry Whispers of Light

Gentle snowflakes kiss the ground,
In a hush, the world awaits,
Whispers of the cold and bright,
Nature spins her magic plates.

Every breath a puffs of white,
Carried softly on the breeze,
Frosted leaves and glimmering Pines,
Sway like dancers among the trees.

In the twilight, shadows play,
A soft glow enchants the sight,
Whispered promises of spring,
In the depths of winter's night.

Footprints fade in powder snow,
Paths unknown they lead away,
Yet in this tranquil, frozen dream,
Hope and warmth will find their way.

Through wintry nights and frosty days,
We gather light, we share the glow,
In whispered dreams, we hold on tight,
As seasons change, we learn and grow.

Winter's Delicate Touch

White blankets cover the ground,
Whispers in the frosty air.
Trees wear coats of crystal lace,
Nature sleeps, a dream laid bare.

Footsteps crunch on icy paths,
Breath like smoke in morning light.
Snowflakes dance in quiet skies,
Softly falling, pure and bright.

The world holds its breath in stillness,
Time slows down beneath the frost.
Glowing lanterns flicker softly,
In this season, warmth is lost.

Children laugh and sled away,
Noses red from winter's chill.
Building snowmen, bright and bold,
Moments captured, time stands still.

As night falls, the stars are bright,
Cold and clear, a velvet dome.
Winter's beauty wraps the earth,
In this magic, we find home.

Prismatic Whispers

In the garden, colors bloom,
Every petal soft and bright.
Sunlight dances on the leaves,
Painting shadows with its light.

The breeze carries whispers sweet,
Songs of nature on the air.
Butterflies float, free and wild,
Fluttering without a care.

Rainbows arch through gentle rains,
Kissing drops that nurture ground.
Vibrant hues in every glance,
Life, in layers, does abound.

Nature's palette, rich and bold,
Tapestries in every bloom.
Every layer tells a tale,
Of joy and love that still loom.

As day fades, colors blend soft,
Crimson skies that fade to night.
Stars peek through the velvet dark,
Promising the dawn's first light.

Hush of Glimmering Frost

Morning breaks with icy breath,
Frost paints windows, gleaming bright.
Silent streets embrace the dawn,
Wrapped in hush, asleep from night.

Each breath feathery in the air,
Nature whispers tales untold.
Glimmering frost on silver grass,
A hidden world of beauty bold.

Footprints left on powdered ground,
Stories traced where shadows lie.
Underneath the crystal veil,
Winter's magic drifts on high.

Branches wear their icy crowns,
Sparkling jewels on every tree.
Quiet moments linger long,
In this world, we find the key.

As dusk descends with shadow's hand,
Stars begin to twinkle bright.
Wrapped in frost, the earth will sleep,
Awaiting morning's gentle light.

Frozen Jewels at Dawn

The horizon glows in pinks,
Morning breaks with tender grace.
Frozen jewels, a glinting sight,
Nature's art in this vast space.

Crystal shards on every branch,
Shimmering like stars on earth.
Dewdrops glisten in new light,
Each moment filled with rebirth.

Silence reigns across the fields,
A canvas white and pure as snow.
Birdsong greets the waking day,
In harmony, life starts to flow.

A soft hush, the world serene,
Wrapped in winter's tender hold.
As day unfolds, warmth soon calls,
In every heart, a story told.

Sunrise paints the world anew,
Embers of the night give way.
Frozen jewels melt to dreams,
As dawn unveils another day.

Moonlit Frost Bites

Beneath the moon's soft glow, shadows dance,
The icy breath whispers, a cold romance.
Each crystal formed in night's gentle embrace,
Holds secrets of winter's delicate grace.

Stars twinkle like diamonds in the night,
The world sleeps silent, wrapped in pure white.
Frost kisses the ground, a delicate art,
Nature's cold beauty, a work of the heart.

Footprints trace stories on frozen streams,
While frostbitten air fuels the night's dreams.
Branches adorned with a shimmering coat,
Nature sings softly, a timeless note.

The chill of the night evokes a sweet thrill,
As winter's breath lingers, crisp and still.
In this moonlit realm, time drifts like a stream,
Awash in the glow, life feels like a dream.

With every blink, the dawn starts to creep,
A promise of warmth, while the world stays asleep.
Yet for this fleeting moment, let it last,
In the grip of the frost, we're held to the past.

Nature's Glittering Veil

Dewdrops sparkle like jewels on the grass,
Morning sun rises, a golden mass.
Whispers of wind through the vibrant leaves,
Nature's soft song, a tale that weaves.

Flowers bloom bright, dressed in colors bold,
Petals unfolding, secrets untold.
In this sacred space, life begins anew,
Every blossom and bud, a world to pursue.

Birds take flight in a chorus of cheer,
Their melodies dance, so sweet to the ear.
Glittering sunlight upon every stream,
Nature's embrace feels like a warm dream.

Mountains stand tall, their majesty clear,
Guardians of time, with wisdom sincere.
Under the azure, our spirits entwine,
Beneath nature's veil, our souls brightly shine.

In the still of the woods, peace can be found,
As whispers of life play a soft, gentle sound.
In every petal, in every tree,
Nature's glittering veil calls out to be free.

Glacial Echoes

In the heart of the ice, whispers reside,
Ancient stories of time frozen inside.
Echoes of labor from ages gone by,
Resound in the silence beneath the sky.

Crystal formations reflect what once was,
A glacial history, nature's applause.
Carved by the chill that the mountains breathe,
In every crevice, a tale to bequeath.

The air, crisp and clear, carries a tune,
Of thawing landscapes under the warm moon.
Frosty exhalations meet sun's gentle rays,
Awakening life in a dance of soft plays.

Wander the fields where ice meets the earth,
In every footstep, there's magic, there's mirth.
Listen for echoes, let them be your guide,
Through glacial realms where wonders abide.

As seasons shift, and the frost starts to fade,
The stories of ice will never degrade.
For glacial echoes, though still as a glance,
Whisper of time in nature's grand dance.

Frosted Petals of Dawn

As morning breaks, a new day arises,
Frosted petals unveil nature's surprises.
Glistening softly, they catch the first light,
Waking the world from a slumber of night.

The chill of the air dances on skin,
While gentle sunbeams coax warmth to begin.
Each blossom adorned with a crystalline sheen,
Tells tales of the night, of the peaceful serene.

Whispers of breeze float through leafy trees,
Carrying secrets on fragrant, soft pleas.
The garden awakens, a canvas so bright,
A palette of colors emerging in sight.

Frost lingers softly on grass blades anew,
Transforming the ordinary, a glittering view.
Each droplet reflects a universe wide,
In this moment of magic, let joy be our guide.

With every petal, the dawn starts to shine,
In nature's embrace, our spirits align.
Frosted memories turn into sweet grace,
As day welcomes life in this beautiful space.

Radiant Pathways of the Frozen World

In twilight's glow, the snowflakes dance,
A shimmering path, a winter's trance.
Soft whispers echo through silent trees,
Nature's cradle, swaying with ease.

Footprints linger on the frosty ground,
A world transformed, where dreams abound.
Beneath the stars, the icebirds sing,
Melodies of joy that the cold can bring.

Glowing lanterns in the night take flight,
Guiding wanderers with flickering light.
Each step forward, a story untold,
In the heart of winter, brave and bold.

With every breath, the air tastes pure,
A fleeting moment, serene and sure.
Radiant beauty all around shines,
In frozen pathways, where magic divine.

The night deepens, but souls ignite,
In radiant pathways that promise light.
Through cold and stillness, heartbeat and sound,
The frozen world waits, enchantingly found.

Icicle's Elegy in Dusk's Embrace

Hanging in silence, pure icicles weep,
In dusk's soft embrace, secrets they keep.
Frayed edges twinkle in fading light,
Silent witnesses of day turning night.

Each drop a story, a memory held,
Of gentle whispers where shadows meld.
A frozen tear on a ledge so still,
An elegy told by the night's chill will.

Fleeting moments of warmth find their end,
As icy fingers around daylight bend.
In twilight's arms, solitude sings,
The life of the icicle, such beauty brings.

Awash in colors of purple and grey,
The world sighs softly as night takes sway.
Each drop that falls, a final farewell,
In icicle's elegy, a crystalline spell.

Embraced by darkness, yet shining bright,
Icicles guard the secrets of night.
In their reflection, the stories untold,
An endless dance in the winter's cold.

Glittering Layers of the Tundra

Beneath the moon, the tundra gleams,
Layers of frost, like whispered dreams.
Blanketed earth in shimmering white,
A quiet canvas, pure and bright.

Subtle whispers of the northern wind,
Gentle caresses, the cold has sinned.
Every crystal sparkles with pride,
In the depths of silence, beauty does hide.

Footprints etched in a lover's embrace,
Tracing the paths of time and space.
Each step a promise, a memory made,
In glittering layers where dreams cascade.

The aurora dances, ribbons of light,
Painting the sky with hues of delight.
Tundra's magic, forever it weaves,
In shimmering banners that no one believes.

Awake with wonder, we roam and play,
Among the layers where shadows sway.
The glittering whispers of an endless night,
In the tundra's heart, our souls take flight.

Frosted Hues of a Silent Night

In tranquil stillness, the world holds its breath,
Frosted hues blanket the earth with depth.
Each star a jewel in the velvet sky,
An invitation to dream, to fly.

Moonlight weaves through the crystalline trees,
Painting shadows that dance in the breeze.
A stillness settles, the heart beats slow,
In frosted splendor, the night starts to glow.

Whispers of winter embrace the land,
As nature cradles every frosty strand.
Soft is the air, with secrets untold,
In frosted hues, the world unfolds.

The echoing silence, a haunting refrain,
Of beauty found in the cold's sweet pain.
Every flake of snow, a story's delight,
In the frosted hues of a silent night.

As dreams take flight, we wander the scene,
In wonderment of the serene and pristine.
Frosted hues linger, forever they spark,
In the silence of night, we find our heart.

Winter's Whispering Light

Softly falls the winter's snow,
Cloaking earth in purest glow.
Whispers ride on chilly air,
Nature's peace beyond compare.

Trees adorned in frosted white,
Glistening 'neath the pale moonlight.
Stars above begin to gleam,
In this quiet, frozen dream.

Branches bow with heavy grace,
In the stillness, find your place.
Footprints mark the path we take,
Through the silence, hearts awake.

Fires crackle, warmth draws near,
Voices soft, intent to cheer.
Gathered close, the stories flow,
In the light of embers' glow.

Winter's breath, a gentle sigh,
Painting scenes beneath the sky.
With each moment, hope takes flight,
In the embrace of winter's light.

Frosted Dreams in Twilight

In twilight's hush, the world stands still,
Frosted dreams the night fulfill.
Shadows dance on icy streams,
Whispers weave through silent dreams.

Glistening stars begin to rise,
Beneath the cloak of dusky skies.
Every breath a misty sigh,
As hopes take wing and quietly fly.

Moonlight spills on frozen ground,
In its glow, pure magic found.
Footsteps soft on powdered white,
Guiding souls through endless night.

Trees stand tall, their branches bare,
Woven tales in frosty air.
Nature's beauty on display,
In a dream that will not sway.

Whispers of the winter breeze,
Carrying the scent of trees.
In this moment, hearts will linger,
Chasing dreams with frost-kissed fingers.

Crystal Reflections of Dawn

Awake with the blush of dawn,
Nature stretches, night is gone.
Crystal dew on blades of grass,
Glimmers sweet as moments pass.

Sunlight spills through frosty air,
Painting skies with shades so rare.
Reflections dance in shades of gold,
Stories new, memories old.

Every ray a bright embrace,
Warming earth, a gentle grace.
Colors burst with vibrant cheer,
In this dawn, the world feels near.

Mountains crowned with glistening light,
Set the scene for day's delight.
Time unfolds, a canvas wide,
In its beauty, hearts abide.

With each breath of morning air,
Hope is born, beyond compare.
In crystal reflections clear,
Every moment treasured dear.

Shimmering Silence of Winter

In the shimmer of winter's glow,
Silence wraps the world in snow.
The night whispers soft and low,
Underneath the stars' soft flow.

Blankets white on every street,
Softening our hurried feet.
Woodland creatures pause and stare,
In the stillness of the air.

Moonbeams dance on frosted lakes,
Sparkling light that gently wakes.
Every corner, hush embraced,
In the magic, time is chased.

Hearts find solace in the night,
Wrapped in peace, a pure delight.
Snowflakes fall like whispered dreams,
Woven with the moonlight beams.

Feel the chill that wraps around,
In this quiet, love is found.
With each breath, a promise made,
In winter's silence, hopes parade.

Ethereal Trails in Frozen Spaces

In twilight's grasp, silence reigns,
Footprints trace where time remains.
The stars above, like whispers glow,
In frozen realms where shadows flow.

Beneath the sky, a quiet dance,
The moonlight weaves its silver trance.
Ethereal paths of crisp, cool air,
In solitude, the heart lays bare.

Whispers of snowflakes softly fall,
Painting white on nature's tall.
Each breath a mist, a fleeting dream,
In stillness, the world starts to seem.

Branches glisten with icy grace,
Nature's art in this sacred space.
Through the dark, a journey calls,
On ethereal trails, the spirit crawls.

A symphony of winter's kiss,
In frozen echoes, find your bliss.
With every step, a tranquil sigh,
In frozen spaces, let thoughts fly.

Scatterings of Shimmer

In the dawn, a sparkle drapes,
Nature wakes, the beauty shapes.
Golden rays on petals lay,
A dance of light to greet the day.

Glistening dew on blades of grass,
Moments fleeting, time will pass.
Each shimmer tells a silent tale,
Stories borne on the softest gale.

Scattered beams in morning's haze,
Illuminate the woodland's ways.
With every glance, a precious find,
Whispers of light, embracing the mind.

As sunlight kisses every hue,
Colors blend in bright debut.
Scatterings of shimmer arise,
Bringing magic beneath the skies.

From dawn to dusk, twinkles play,
In every moment, a chance to stay.
The universe in each small gleam,
Weaving dreams within a dream.

Luminous Veils of the Morn

Emerging light through softest mist,
The dawn unfolds with a gentle twist.
Luminous veils stretch wide and far,
Awakening hopes beneath the star.

Golden hues in the tranquil air,
Whispers of grace, a tender prayer.
Nature's canvas, painted bright,
In luminous veils, the day takes flight.

Each sunbeam dances on the stream,
Reflecting dreams in morning's beam.
Where petals blush and new life breathes,
Hope springs forth, as nature weaves.

In the chorus of the waking world,
Each note a story softly unfurled.
Graceful motions of life arise,
In luminous veils, our spirits fly.

A promise held in the morning's grace,
Casting shadows that gently embrace.
In the twilight of the day reborn,
We find ourselves in luminous morn.

Frosty Symphony in Blue

Beneath a sky of cobalt hue,
The world unfolds, a frosty view.
Icy notes in the air so clear,
Nature whispers, drawing near.

The wind's sweet song, a lullaby,
Through winter's breath, the echoes sigh.
Frosted branches, a crystal choir,
Together we revel in winter's fire.

In tranquil stillness, time stands still,
The magic of frost begins to thrill.
A symphony of chill and grace,
Frosty wonders in this space.

As twilight drapes its velvet shroud,
The night unfolds with a mystic crowd.
In each blue shadow, stories loom,
A frosty symphony's balmy gloom.

With every breath, a chill ingrain,
In the silence, beauty's reign.
In frosty realms, we find our song,
Embraced by wonders, we belong.

Sparkling Horizons

Beneath the vast and endless sky,
The sun ignites a golden blaze.
Rays of light, they dance and fly,
Painting dreams in endless ways.

Mountains rise with snowy crowns,
Echoes of a distant song.
Rivers weave through silent towns,
Where nature's wonders all belong.

Fields of green, where daisies bloom,
Whispers of the wind so light.
In their grace, there's no more gloom,
Just the warmth of pure delight.

Stars will twinkle in the night,
Guiding hearts with gentle grace.
Every shadow, every light,
Creates a canvas, wide and base.

Horizons sparkle, dreams take flight,
In the twilight's soft embrace.
Chasing visions, bold and bright,
In the skies, we find our place.

Chilling Radiance

In winter's clasp, the world stands still,
Whispers glide on frigid air.
Every breath a ghostly thrill,
Shimmering secrets everywhere.

Frosted branches dance on trees,
Veils of silver hanging low.
In the silence, hearts find ease,
Chilling radiance starts to glow.

Moonlight spills like whispers soft,
Casting shadows long and deep.
With each glimmer, spirits loft,
Awake within a tranquil sleep.

The fire flickers in the hearth,
Warmth against the bitter cold.
Every crackle tells a story,
Woven threads of tales retold.

In this glow, we find our peace,
Moments frozen, yet alive.
As we breathe, the world can cease,
Chilling radiance helps us thrive.

Veils of Ice and Starfire

Night descends with icy breath,
Veils of ice cloak every sight.
Whispers linger, threads of death,
Stars ignite the endless night.

Through the frost, the shadows creep,
Survival in a bitter land.
In the silence, secrets keep,
Nature's beauty, bold and grand.

Crystals form in moonlit gaze,
Reflecting dreams from distant shores.
In the dark, the heart ablaze,
Finding solace, opening doors.

As dawn meets the frozen ground,
Flames of starfire gently rise.
In the stillness, hope is found,
Echoes dance beneath the skies.

Veils of ice and starfire bright,
Tales of wonder in the air.
Life awakens with the light,
In this magic, we shall dare.

Flickering Lanterns of Frost

In the darkness, lanterns glow,
Each a flicker, soft and warm.
Guiding souls where shadows flow,
Amidst the cold, we find our charm.

Beneath the stars, like dreams untold,
Wisps of light in winter's veil.
Stories whispered, brave and bold,
A spark ignites within the pale.

Trees adorned with icy lace,
Crystals shine with frosty smile.
Every corner, every space,
Holds a magic all the while.

With each step, the night unfolds,
Paths illuminated, clear and bright.
In our hearts, warmth gently scolds,
Revealing beauty in the night.

Flickering lanterns dance in glee,
Echoes of a joyful song.
In their glow, we find the key,
To a world where we belong.

Gleaming Touch of Winter's Breath

The trees wear coats of glistening white,
Stars twinkle softly, glowing bright.
Whispers of ice in the chilly air,
Nature sleeps with a tranquil stare.

Footsteps crunch on the powdery ground,
A world of silence, peace profound.
Snowflakes dance like a gentle breeze,
Winter's touch puts the heart at ease.

Breezes sing through the frosted pines,
In every heartbeat, winter shines.
The moon illuminates the quiet night,
Casting shadows in soft, silver light.

Clarity shines in the frosty glow,
Each breath is visible, slow, and low.
Branches bow under snow's gentle weight,
Winter whispers, it's never too late.

As night falls with its icy charm,
We are cradled in winter's warm.
The world is hushed, a magic spell,
In winter's breath, all is well.

Sparkling Secrets of the Frost

Beneath the dawn, the frost unfolds,
A tapestry in silver and gold.
Each crystal glimmers in morning light,
Revealing secrets of the night.

Patterns weave on the windowpane,
Echoes of whispers from the plain.
Nature's art in dazzling hue,
A hidden world, fresh and new.

Frosted breaths rise in the air,
Mysteries linger, soft and rare.
Trees in gowns of diaphanous white,
Celebrate the beauty, pure delight.

Gentle hands of winter trace,
Delicate lines that time can't erase.
In frozen tears, warmth survives,
Sparkling secrets bloom and thrive.

As day unfolds, the magic stays,
In every glimmer, a thousand ways.
Nature's whispers unveil its trust,
Sparkling secrets, a world of dust.

Glistening Canopy of White

Beneath the sky, a canvas wide,
Fields of snow where dreams reside.
Cottony clouds drift and sway,
Above the world in soft decay.

The trees stand tall, a guardian's role,
Encased in winter's frosty shoal.
Icicles dangle like crystal spears,
A testament to the passing years.

Snowflakes fall like whispered notes,
Carried gently by the coats.
They settle down, a silent cheer,
Creating beauty year by year.

In this glistening canopy high,
Every sigh echoes a lullaby.
The world beneath with grace complies,
Under the gaze of muted skies.

Shimmering worlds beckon us near,
In every flake, a wish sincere.
Nature wraps us in her embrace,
In white serenity, we find our place.

Frosty Serenade at Nightfall

As shadows deepen with twilight's kiss,
The world transforms into pure bliss.
Frosty serenades fill the night,
Under the stars, everything feels right.

The moon's soft glow dances on the snow,
Whispers of winter begin to flow.
A gentle tune in the crisping air,
Nature sings of beauty rare.

The night winds carry a soothing sound,
Lullabies blanket the sleeping ground.
With every breath, the stillness warms,
Wrapped in winter's charming arms.

Beneath the stars, dreams take their flight,
In frosty shadows, hearts feel light.
Every flake that falls is a note,
In the symphony of winter, we float.

As night embraces the world so wide,
In frosty serenity, we're intertwined.
A serenade, peaceful and clear,
Through winter's breath, love draws us near.

Luminescent Chill

In twilight's glow, the world pulsates,
A whispering breeze that gently waits.
Stars awaken in the velvet night,
Casting shadows that dance in delight.

Moonlit paths where dreams entwine,
Silent echoes of a love divine.
Each breath hangs like frost in the air,
A tranquil beauty that none can compare.

Winter's heartbeat amidst the still,
The universe wrapped in a tranquil thrill.
Soft glimmers twinkle on crystal pane,
A fleeting moment, both sweet and plain.

Frosty fingers trace the window's edge,
Nature's artistry, a silent pledge.
With every blink, the night unfolds,
Stories captured in halos of gold.

In this luminescent chill we find,
A tapestry woven by fate and time.
Each shimmering moment, a tale to tell,
In the heart of winter, all is well.

A Tapestry of Winter's Touch

Snowflakes dance on the breath of night,
Whispers of silver in soft moonlight.
Branches adorned in a gown of white,
Nature's treasure, a pure delight.

Blankets of silence gently enfold,
Stories of winter begin to be told.
Crystals glitter as shadows weave,
In this stillness, we dare believe.

Footprints echo on a frost-tipped lane,
Memories linger, a soothing refrain.
Each step a promise, each breath a sigh,
Beneath the vast and endless sky.

In twilight's embrace, the stars align,
An endless journey, a quest divine.
Wrapped in the chill of a moonlit hush,
Time stands still in the gentle rush.

A tapestry woven with love and care,
In winter's warmth, we find our share.
Every heartbeat, a thread in the seam,
A wondrous existence, a shared dream.

Celestial Twinkle in the Cold

Under the dome of a starry expanse,
Snowflakes pirouette as night does dance.
Celestial bodies gleam bright and clear,
Whispers of magic fill the cold air.

Frosted branches bow in graceful sway,
Acknowledging night and the coming day.
Constellations twinkle with secrets to share,
Enchanting our hearts with a love laid bare.

Each star a wish, a distant light,
Guiding our dreams into the night.
In the chill, we find solace and peace,
As the universe wraps us, never to cease.

Moments linger like dew on a leaf,
In this cosmic calm, we find belief.
Frost-kissed whispers of hopes yet to bloom,
Emanating warmth against the night's gloom.

The cold hugs tight, yet we stand bold,
In the heart of winter, stories unfold.
A celestial twinkle, our hearts ignite,
Bringing the shadows a reason for light.

Frost-Kissed Murmurs

Whispers of winter, soft and low,
Frost-kissed secrets beneath the snow.
Gentle breezes breathe through the trees,
As silence lingers in moments of ease.

The world wrapped in a glistening shroud,
Nature yet quiet, yet fiercely proud.
Each flake a story, unique and pure,
In the stillness, a magic we endure.

Embers of twilight, fading light,
Stars unveil in the coming night.
Murmurs of love dance on icy breath,
In the cradle of winter, life lingers yet.

A canvas painted in hues of white,
Every shadow a tale in the night.
Frost-kissed whispers trickle like streams,
Woven together in delicate dreams.

Time slows down, as if to embrace,
Moments captured in winter's grace.
In these frosted murmurs, we find our song,
A symphony played where we all belong.

Ethereal Sparkle of Chill

Beneath the moon's soft glow,
The night whispers its spell.
Chill air dances lightly,
In echoes where shadows dwell.

Stars twinkle like secrets,
In a velvet sky so deep.
The frost-kissed world awakens,
While the weary dreamers sleep.

Crystals form in silence,
Each breath a fleeting sigh.
Nature's breath, a moment,
In stillness, time drifts by.

Winds weave through the branches,
A lullaby sung low.
Ethereal sparkle surrounds,
In a winter's gentle flow.

Whispers of the cold night,
With warmth that flickers bright.
In the heart of frost and night,
Lies a magic, pure delight.

Diamonds on a White Canvas

Snowflakes dance and shimmer,
Bright jewels on a field of white.
A canvas draped in stillness,
Catches morning's golden light.

Each step leaves a footprint,
Crafted in the glistening frost.
Nature's art appears untouched,
In wonders that never are lost.

Trees wear coats of silver,
Adorned by winter's grace.
An icy crown of beauty,
In this quiet, sacred space.

The world feels like magic,
With secrets held so dear.
Diamonds on a white canvas,
Whispers of the coming year.

Beneath the wide expanse,
Dreams glimmer with delight.
In the soft embrace of winter,
Every moment feels just right.

A Dance of Frost and Light

Morning breaks in silence,
As shadows stretch and grow.
Frost begins its twinkling,
In a world wrapped in snow.

A dance of soft reflections,
On branches tall and bare.
Light kisses the frozen ground,
In a delicate affair.

Each ray a gentle whisper,
In chorus with the chill.
The air is filled with magic,
A landscape, calm and still.

Sparkling underfoot,
Nature's crystals glisten bright.
The world transforms in beauty,
In this dance of frost and light.

Every breath a frosty plume,
In the hush of winter's bill.
A spectacle of nature,
A timeless winter thrill.

Enchanted Crystals Underfoot

Beneath the arch of branches,
A tapestry unfolds.
Crystals gleam like secrets,
In stories yet untold.

Each step brings a crunch of magic,
A symphony of ice.
Enchanted paths invite us,
With whispers soft and nice.

The world is wrapped in wonder,
Each corner hides a dream.
A delicate reflection,
In sunlight's gentle beam.

Every shadow dances lightly,
On carpets made of white.
Enchanted crystals beckon,
In the warmth of winter's light.

As we wander through this realm,
The heart begins to soar.
Underfoot, pure enchantment,
A winter we adore.

Illuminated Silence

In the hush of night, stars gleam,
Whispers of shadows softly weave.
The world is wrapped in a dream,
In this calm, we truly believe.

Moonlight dances on the ground,
Casting silver on the trees.
In this beauty, peace is found,
Carried gently by the breeze.

Footsteps fade on the cold earth,
Echoes lost in the still air.
Each moment speaks of rebirth,
Silence sings, a sweet affair.

Eyes closed tight, we drift away,
To a realm where thoughts take flight.
In the night, the heart will sway,
Embracing the depth of light.

A soft sigh in the deep night,
Hearts met under the starlit dome.
In this glow, everything feels right,
Illuminated silence, our home.

Radiance in Every Flake

Falling softly, a silent grace,
Snowflakes twirl, each one unique.
Sparkling jewels in winter's embrace,
Nature's art, so pure, mystique.

A dance of white across the ground,
Whispers of magic in the air.
Each flake tells a story profound,
Of fleeting moments, light as air.

Glistening on branches, a sight to behold,
The world transformed, wrapped in white.
A canvas of stories yet untold,
Filling hearts with pure delight.

Children laugh, making their mark,
Snowmen rise, and angels spread.
In this bright world, there's a spark,
Where joy and wonder are widespread.

With every flake, winter glows,
Radiance in each gentle fall.
A blanket of wonder that softly grows,
In the stillness, we hear the call.

When Winter Becomes a Canvas

A palette of white, the world transformed,
Brushstrokes of frost paint the trees.
In silence, the landscape is warmed,
By the breath of the chill in the breeze.

Each branch a stroke, each flake a hue,
The sky wears a blanket, pure and bright.
Nature's masterpiece comes into view,
As the day bows down to the night.

Footprints echo on fresh fallen snow,
Stories etched in the frosty air.
A canvas where time moves slow,
Moments captured, beyond compare.

The sun casts a glow on the white expanse,
Painting shadows in deep blue.
In the stillness, life takes a chance,
When winter unveils a world so new.

As stars twinkle against the dark,
The canvas glows with a gentle light.
In this season, we find the spark,
Winter's wonder, a pure delight.

Enchantments of a Crystal Dawn

Awake to the shimmer of morning's breath,
A crystal dawn awakens the day.
The world, adorned in frost's caress,
Sparkles bright in the sun's soft play.

Each blade of grass a jeweled strand,
Every tree clad in diamonds rare.
Nature whispers with a gentle hand,
Enchantments linger in the air.

In the stillness, magic unfurls,
Birds sing sweetly, greeting the light.
As the sun rises, the world twirls,
Embracing the beauty, pure and bright.

Clouds dance lightly on the horizon,
Cascading colors, a painter's stroke.
In this moment, hearts align on,
The canvas where dreams invoke.

With every ray, new hopes arise,
In the glow of a brand-new morn.
For in each dawn, the spirit flies,
Enchantments of grace, reborn.

Shimmering Stars on a Frosted Night

Stars shimmer bright in the cold sky,
Whispers of dreams as night drifts by.
Each twinkle dances, a secret gleam,
Carrying wishes from hearts that dream.

The frost paints patterns on icy leaves,
Nature's canvas, the night weaves.
Silvery whispers in the crisp air,
A magical spell, beyond compare.

Underneath this celestial show,
The world sleeps softly, bathed in glow.
A blanket of silence, pure and slight,
Cradled gently in the frosted night.

Icy Veils of Ethereal Light

In the hush of night, a soft allure,
Veils of light weave, calm and pure.
Icy tendrils, the air alive,
Magic whispers, the heart will thrive.

Shadows flicker in the moon's embrace,
Ethereal glow, a celestial grace.
Frosted breath in the chill of air,
Nature's beauty, beyond compare.

Dance of brilliance, cold yet warm,
Under the stars, we find our form.
Strands of silver through darkened hue,
In the night's cradle, dreams come true.

Subtle Glows in a Winter's Dream

Subtle glows in the cold night breeze,
Winter's dream wrapped beneath the trees.
Glistening branches, silver threads weave,
A tapestry born from the warmth we grieve.

Each flake falls softly, a fleeting kiss,
Painting the world with an icy bliss.
Gentle murmurs of winds that sigh,
In this moment, we learn to fly.

The glow is quiet, the night serene,
In winter's arms, we find our dream.
Wrapped in shimmer, the heart beats fast,
In this frozen beauty, we are cast.

Frosted Nocturne of a Glistening Earth

In the frost's embrace, the world aglow,
Whispers of winter faintly flow.
Nocturnal songs of shimmering light,
Carry us gently through the night.

Crystal droplets on silk-clad trees,
Harmonies linger upon the breeze.
A frosted nocturne, sweet and rare,
Painting the earth with delicate care.

Underneath the vast, starry sprawl,
Each note resounds, a mesmerizing call.
Embraced by the chill, hearts find their worth,
In the frosted beauty of the glistening earth.

Whispering Winds Through Silver Pines

The silver pines sway gently,
Their whispers fill the air.
Underneath the pale moonlight,
Secrets dance without a care.

Branches creak with soft laughter,
As the night cools down with grace.
Every gust a hidden story,
Leaves flutter in a soft embrace.

Stars peek through the canopy,
Winking in the twilight glow.
Nature's symphony is playing,
A melody we all know.

In the hush of twilight's charm,
I walk the forest's gentle way.
With every breath, I find solace,
In the night, my heart can stay.

The silver pines hold whispers tight,
Each tale wrapped in a sigh.
In this enchanted, soothing space,
I listen to the winds fly by.

Luminous Echoes on Icy Paths

Beneath a sky of shimmering stars,
I tread upon the frozen ground.
Icy paths reflect the night,
Luminous echoes all around.

Footprints linger in the frost,
Each step a moment caught in time.
The night air sparkles with crystal light,
A scene composed like a whispered rhyme.

Winds caress my glowing cheeks,
As I wander through the still.
The echo of the night surrounds,
Nature's peace, my heart to fill.

Whispers of the moonlight trace,
Patterns on the gleaming ice.
In the depth of winter's grip,
I find warmth in every slice.

Luminous echoes guide me home,
Where comfort waits in soft embrace.
On icy paths beneath the stars,
I rest in this tranquil place.

Glowing Embers of the Cold

In the hearth, the embers glow,
Casting warmth in the darkened room.
Outside, the winter winds do blow,
But here, within, we banish gloom.

Softly crackling, flames do dance,
Twilight paints the walls with fire.
Each flicker offers a second chance,
As shadows twist and dreams conspire.

We gather close to share our tales,
Voices blend with the flames' soft song.
In the heart of winter, love prevails,
With glowing embers, we all belong.

The night sky heavy with its cloak,
Beneath the stars, our spirits rise.
In each warmth, a promise spoke,
Through whispered hopes and tender sighs.

Glowing embers of the cold,
Radiant joy in a quiet space.
Together, we cherish stories told,
In this warmth, we find our place.

Shining Traces of Winter's Tale

Snowflakes twirl in the frosty breeze,
A dance of whispers through the air.
Each flake a story, a memory seized,
In winter's hush, we find our prayer.

The world adorned in sparkling white,
Each branch dressed in crystal peace.
Nature's canvas, pure delight,
Traces of beauty that never cease.

Moonlight bathes the silent ground,
As shadows play among the trees.
A solemn oath in silence bound,
Winter's tale floats on the freeze.

Footprints mark the snowy path,
A journey shared in soft retreat.
In laughter's echo, feel the warmth,
A subtle joy in every beat.

Shining traces of winter's grace,
Remind us life is full and bright.
In every moment, find your place,
Enjoy the magic of the night.

Shining Frost upon a Whispered Night

In silent shadows soft and white,
A glimmer dances, pure delight.
The stars above, they twinkle bright,
Embracing winter's gentle night.

Beneath the moon's caress we stand,
With frosted dreams at our command.
The world adorned, as if planned,
Each flake a secret, hand in hand.

A whispered chill, a breath so light,
The air aglow, a wondrous sight.
Nature's breath, the frozen air tight,
We wander forth, hearts feeling right.

The branches hold their crystal lace,
In quiet gardens, we find our place.
As icy whispers leave no trace,
We lose ourselves in winter's grace.

So let us walk this peaceful lane,
With frosty fingers, free of pain.
For in this night, all dreams remain,
A whispered world, in joy's refrain.

Chilled Grace Beneath the Glimmering Sky

The sky, a canvas painted blue,
With silver clouds that drift and strew.
A chilly breeze whispers anew,
Embracing us in nature's cue.

Beneath the stars, our spirits soar,
In frosty air, we yearn for more.
The evening calls, it opens doors,
To winter wonders we explore.

With each soft step on snowy ground,
A peaceful hush is all around.
In frozen beauty, love is found,
As nature wraps us, safe and sound.

The world, a realm of glistening dreams,
In shimmering light, the moonlight beams.
We dance in shadows, silent themes,
As winter weaves its icy schemes.

In every breath, a frosty trace,
The chill of night, a warm embrace.
We find our joy, our rightful place,
Beneath the sky, in winter's grace.

Glimmer and Glaze of a Winter's Day

The dawn unfolds with glistening hues,
A world adorned with frosty views.
Each branch and leaf, in diamond dues,
Reflecting light, the heart renews.

Among the pines, a quiet glow,
As soft winds weave the flakes that flow.
In every turn, the chill will show,
A dance of nature, slow and low.

The sun ascends, a gentle light,
It warms the earth, dispelling night.
With glimmering glaze, the world feels right,
In winter's hush, we find our flight.

The air is crisp, the sky so wide,
In snowy paths, our dreams abide.
With every step, we feel the tide,
Of winter's magic, love our guide.

So cherish now this fleeting day,
With glimmer and glaze that come to play.
In winter's heart, we find our way,
To treasure moments, come what may.

Celestial Worldwide Shrink

In evening's glow, the heavens shrink,
A vast expanse where stars still wink.
The world below begins to think,
In quiet wonder, we all sync.

The fabric of the night unfolds,
A tapestry of stories told.
In cosmic whispers, dreams so bold,
We find our place amidst the cold.

Each twinkle shines, a distant spark,
Illuminating paths in dark.
As stardust falls, we leave our mark,
In unity, we won't embark.

The night is deep, the silence grand,
In tranquil moments, hand in hand.
With every wish, a heart will stand,
In love's embrace, we understand.

So let us gaze at skies so wide,
With celestial grace, we will abide.
In every star, our dreams confide,
As winter holds the world inside.

Frosted Lace in the Moonlight

Delicate ice on window panes,
Whispers of winter's cold refrains.
Moonlight dancing on frosted ground,
Nature's beauty in silence found.

Trees adorned in shimmering white,
A scene that glows in soft twilight.
Each branch draped in crystal lace,
Embracing the stillness, we find grace.

Footprints trace a path so pure,
A journey into night's allure.
Stars peek through a veil so thin,
Where dreams begin, and wonders spin.

Silent shadows, secrets kept,
Under the moon, the world has slept.
In this tranquil embrace of night,
Frosted lace shines, a lovely sight.

Nature whispers, softly calls,
As frosted lace like magic falls.
Every breath a cloud, a sigh,
In the moonlight, our spirits fly.

Illuminated Pathways of Chill

Through the frost, a pathway glows,
Where icy breath of winter blows.
Lanterns flicker in the night,
Guiding hearts toward warmth and light.

Silvery trails of shimmering frost,
On a journey where warmth is lost.
Every step a dance of grace,
In the chill, we find our place.

Boughs heavy with snowflakes cling,
Silence woven in the winter's string.
Each moment shines with glacial flair,
As the world beneath is laid bare.

Echoes of laughter under stars,
In the cold, we've come so far.
Light spills softly, gentle sway,
Illuminated pathways lead the way.

In the crisp air, friendships grow,
Through the chill, our spirits flow.
Hand in hand, we journey forth,
Illuminated by winter's worth.

Glistening Typhoon's Embrace

Winds that howl with a tempest's might,
Nature dances in wild delight.
Torrents sweep across the shore,
Glistening chaos, forevermore.

Raindrops shimmer under the sky,
A spectacle where wild hopes fly.
The sea swells in a frothy rage,
Each wave a story, a vibrant page.

Lightning flashes, thunder roars,
As the tempest opens its doors.
In the swirl, we find our dreams,
Caught in nature's wild extremes.

Branches sway in the storm's tight grip,
A zany twist on fate's strange trip.
Yet in the heart of fierce embrace,
Glistening beauty finds its place.

After the storm, a calm descends,
Nature's journey never ends.
From the chaos, peace breaks free,
In the embrace of the raging sea.

Frigid Patterns of Glowing Joy

Winters' breath shapes the earth anew,
As patterns weave through skies so blue.
Frigid air, but hearts are warm,
In the chill, we find our charm.

Snowflakes dance like tiny stars,
Each unique, like dreams of ours.
They glisten bright on frozen land,
A canvas made by nature's hand.

Footsteps crunch in the crisp delight,
As laughter echoes through the night.
In this wonder, we laugh and play,
Frigid patterns guide our way.

Every moment, magic grows,
In the stillness, the joy flows.
With each breath, the cold ignite,
Patterns glowing, pure and bright.

Together we craft our memories,
In the cold, we feel the breeze.
Frigid patterns of glowing joy,
As winter's heart we all employ.